AF226134

Brawler of the Pen

by J. D. 'Jet' Jones
with artwork by
Katie Jones
Min Jones
Eva Luther
Kath Pemble
Earl Robinson

A catalogue record for this book is available from the National Library of Australia

One of the things I like best about "Bush Poetry" is the great diversity of our writers and the differing experiences, talents and creativity they bring to the table. From my childhood days, hanging on every word, as my father read me the poems of Banjo and Will Ogilvie, through to the present day where a rapidly changing world has brought a decidedly more 'urban feel' and a high comedy content to Bush Poetry

I met Jet Jones at The Hughenden Country Music Festival where I was officiating as a judge and Jet was displaying his talents as a singer. When he politely inquired if he would be able to join me in performing some of his poems at the 'Poets Breakfast', I found myself wondering just what he would have to offer.

I was very pleasantly surprised, for despite the fact that he had acquitted himself very well in the various 'singing' categories, it was obvious to me that his 'real' talent resided in his ability to write and perform Bush Poetry.

Jet has the ability and common sense to write from the heart, about things he has known and lived. His poetry is raw and authentic, there is no slick delivery from someone who has researched their subject matter, he knows what he is writing about. He displays the ability to paint word pictures vividly so that the listener or reader is transported into the story. Listening to him perform I found myself grabbing a handful of plaited red-hide rein, feeling the sweat streaking the fine dust on my face and enjoying the power of a good stock horse as he raced after a bolting steer. Any writer who has the ability to evoke these emotions, or memories in a reader, has, in my opinion, truly 'won his spurs'.

I recommend this book to the reader without hesitation, within its pages you will get a unique insight into rural Australia form the pen of a man who has truly lived the life he writes about. A life which, unfortunately, is quickly being swallowed by technology and the modern world, which makes the bush poetry of Jet Jones even more important.

Gary Fogarty
Award Winning Bush Poet
www.garyfogarty.com

'Peaceful Dreams,' watercolour pencil on paper by Eva Luther

Table of Contents

Remember the Days

Remember the days when we rose at dawn,
With the early light, on a winters morn.
When the frost broke cold with the breaking day,
We saddled our horses and rode away.
Remember those days.

Remember the times when the chopper roared,
Brought the scrubbers from the basalt gorge.
Your horse twitched his ears as the coachers held,
For the game was on that he knew so well.
Remember those times.

Remember the rains that caught you out,
As lighting crashed on the plains about.
The water poured down off your old felt hat,
And you bore the mark of a half-drowned cat.
Remember those rains.

Watercolour on paper by Earl Robinson

Remember the sounds of the gates and chutes.
While you tied the spurs to leather boots.
You wished you drank less and slept some more,
At the cabaret on the night before.
Remember those sounds.

Remember the dust as you worked the draft.
On a black soil plain in the timber yards.
And you couldn't hear half the words you said.
For the deafening roar of a thousand head.
Remember the dust.

'Remember the Days,' charcoal on canvas by Katie Jones

Remember the heat as the mob strung out.
The accursed flies that buzzed about.
Your throat burned dry and your body wet,
Break a drought with your pouring sweat.
Remember the heat.

Remember your swag at as you went to bed,
The pillow soft to your tired head.
And it barely felt like you'd closed your eyes.
Then your clock called out time to rise.
Remember those days.

Oil on canvas by Min Jones

Watercolour on paper by Earl Robinson

Out Where the Good Dogs Lie

Scratched on the side of an old iron tank, near where the old mill lays,
There, next to a cool basalt waterhole, if you ever pass that way
Is the name of a dog buried long ago, from a time that has long past us by.
I wonder how many there in the bush rest? Out where the good dogs lie.

By a tall she oak where the mountains crest, and the rivers, come wet, run fast
Lies the bones of the toughest dog I've ever known in the years since and past.
On the nose of a bull the battle was won, at the cost of a soldier's life.
Up in the hills of that broken range, out where the good dogs lie.

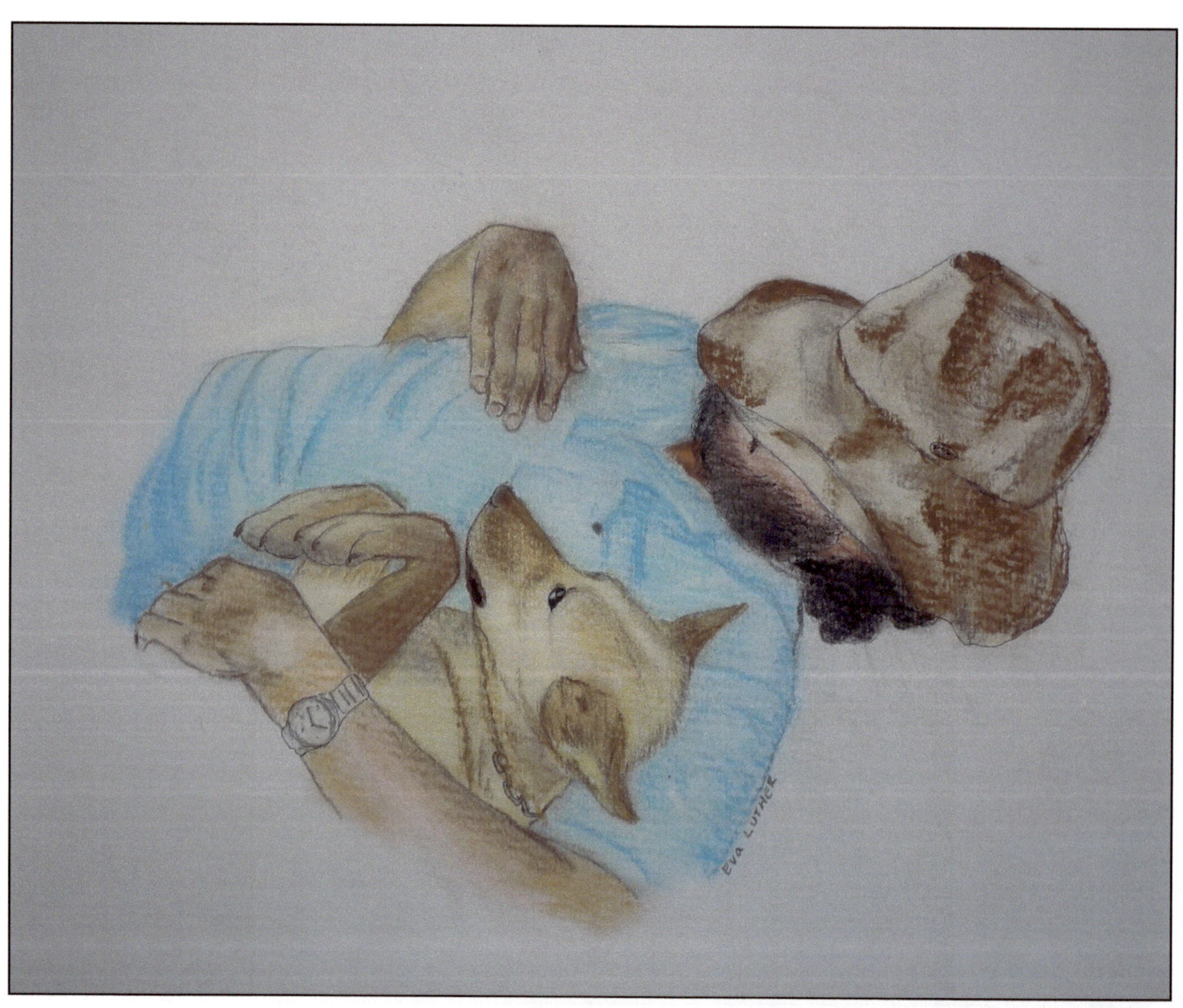

'Afternoon Nap,' watercolour pencils on paper by Eva Luther

There in the shade of a Morten Ash, on the banks of a dry creek bed.
Is where a bitch, as hard as an iron pike, lies her faithful head.
But still, though she's gone, I think on back and I have to crack a smile
At the heart she showed under fire and hoof, out where the good dogs lie.

There's a mound of dirt on a rocky ridge, south of the homestead fence.
Where a black dog from a snake bite gave, his all for his man's defence.
And there on the mound some heather lays, and I often give a sigh.
When I pass that way on a winter's day, out where the good dogs lie.

'You've Been a Good Dog,' charcoal on canvas by Katie Jones

Whether red or blue or black matters not – tall, thin, or short and stout –
When the work is hard and the action's quick and men are few about.
Where those that will beat those that don't, not name of his dam or sire,
Where the hard working dog is king, out where the good dogs lie.

Where the tall trees grow on the river banks and ringers ride for mob to yard,
The sweat runs down on the stockman's brow and the western dust blows hard.
Where the dingo calls at night to the yellow moon on the open plains I ride.
There, where we shall forget them not, out where the good dogs lie.

'Protected Pup,' watercolour pencils on paper by Eva Luther

'Reminiscing,' watercolour pencils on paper by Eva Luther

Son of Truly Brave

I went to work up in the Basalt, where the Broken River flows,
In the dark and rocky gorges, where the Black Butt and She Oak grow,
Where the winter frost will bite you and the summer heat will burn,
And the black rock makes you work hard for each dollar that you earn.
So, I went up to Wandovale when I was sixteen years of age,
Back when the station stallion was a horse called Truly Brave.

And the prodigy he sired a type I've so rarely seen or rode,
In the years before and after and the horses I have known.
My brother worked a brown colt, roman-nosed and game of eye,
With shoulders built like granite and his head was held up high.
With hind quarters built to carry on the longest, hardest days,
A testament to horse flesh was this son of Truly Brave.

'Hopeful Clouds on a Dry Land,' oil on canvas by Katie Jones

He soon showed his worth among them as an honest working hack;
He owned a lot of good points but a long way from the crack.
He could put in all the hard yards and more than pull his weight.
Sure, he was a good young stock horse but a long way from a great,
But he had yet to show then us of the steel that he was made,
Out there on the twelve mile flat this son of Truly Brave.

We had walked the mob of bullocks while the pilot scouted in,
But he seemed a little anxious like a rum waited for him.
For I'm sure his skin was cracking and his nerves in need of fuel,
And he bulged them like a mad man and he ran them like a fool
On the last mob, pulled out early, and the bullocks raced away,
So my brother raced to bend them on the son of Truly Brave.

There were two who were between us, so I settled in my place,
As we started cross the blackened rock to follow in the chase.
But those 'good' men who'd told how hard they'd ride in rock,
Struggled on gun horses to even break free from a trot.
So I broke the rules and pulled out, and doubled up the rains,
And rode hard to try to catch up to that son of Truly Brave.

Now the little bay that I was riding was a mare, one of my own.
She had seen a lot of hard miles in the short life she had known.
She was full or hate and savage; she could bite and strike and kick,
And she lived for chasing cattle where the wattle scrubs grew thick.
But she hadn't seen much basalt till I drove her through that plain.
As we rode hard to close the distance, on the son of Truly Brave.

That brown horse raced the stones, like Gunsynd down the track.
The pace he cut was frightening and he never drew the slack.
And onward still I drove my mare, for fast as she could go,
You'd swear I'd breached the gates of hell with Lucifer in tow.
But if Old Nick had chose to chase us in his vilest demon rage,
I hold my doubts he could have caught that son of Truly Brave.

The big horse galloped across the boulders like Pegasus would fly.
Had he had gone and sprouted wings I'd not have been surprised.
I plucked and spurred and doubled, just to try and catch that brown.
But the best it seemed I'd hope for, was not losing too much ground.
So, we charged the open basalt both too hot to feel the pain.
As in vain we tried to close in on the son of Truly Brave.

He hit the racing bullocks where the ground was undermined,
And the tail it broke behind him, but I got there just in time
To swing those charging brahmans as he rang the leaders hard,
To the gateway of the cooler out by the twelve-mile yards.
And we hadn't blown a bullock, not one had got away,
Outmatched in the gallop, by the son of Truly Brave.

The sweat ran from her fetlocks; her right front foot was lame.
And though in time it healed it up, it was never quite the same.
Breathing hard, foam from the bridle, cut from rock and spur,
Like we'd run the pits of Hades, chased by his spotted cur.
But though the brown, he puffed a little, he seemed so much unfazed,
For bred for rock and riding hard, was that son of Truly Brave.

Now many years have passed since then, and horses I have known,
Through mountain range and desert sand to land of ice and snow.
And I've pushed the upmost limits of where man and horse can ride,
On horseflesh likes of Nick and Eden, and the black horse with one eye.
But I've yet to see another one in the black rock to this day.
Could run the holes and basalt, like that son of Truly Brave.

Watercolour on paper by Earl Robinson

Men of the Western Plains

I've lived my life as best I could, up here on the timbered range,
And the coastal life with its muggy heat I've held in much distain.
I've ventured down to the western towns and though myself refrain,
I tip my hat to the men who live out there on the western plains.

The stalwart type is the western man, and he must if he shall remain,
In a land that's seen cattle turn to sheep, then back to beef again.
As he faces droughts, that'll wipe you out and when at last it rains,
His cattle bog in the black soil flats, out there on the western plains.

The winter brings that lazy wind that cuts through your coat and soul,
As it blows and howls cross the open flats where the roly poly rolls.
And he lives in fear of the Pimelea or just twenty points of rain,
That will turn the Flinders grass to black, out there on the western plains.

Watercolour on paper by Earl Robinson

15

A western woman is hard and tough, can toil in the scorchest heat,
But this land she loves is a mistress and at times she must compete.
As she looks around at the open downs and curses her fickle ways,
For the fathers, sons and husbands lost to the charms of the western plains.

But with seasons good, the Mitchell grass in the wind will bend and sway,
At stirrup high with the rolling breeze as vast as an ocean's waves.
The stock grow strong and it won't be long till his bullocks fat again,
And the price he'll get makes us all wish we were men of the western plains.

'Flinders Poppy', acrylic ink on paper by Eva Luther

The Pilot Peter Smith

When the beef slump finally ended, it left places out of hand.
Run down, and overrun, and badly undermanned.
And those who filled the shortfall found themselves in much demand,
In the dawning of the era of the helicopter man.

And some of them were useless, and some seemed to have a gift,
But none I saw were equal to the pilot Peter Smith.

The man became a legend for the things that he could do,
Perched up in the cockpit of his Robbo 22.
Down there north of Clermont where the Balyando flows,
In the Gidgee and the Lancewood and the stands of Brigalow.

Just the right amount of pressure, just the right amount of lift,
Like a surgeon with a scalpel was the pilot Peter Smith.

'Chopper,' charcoal on canvas by Katie Jones

We awed in admiration how he spun those blades about,
And often had to wonder he never turned it inside out.
Putting cattle into coaches, putting scrubbers into yards:
How he made it look so easy, what others found so hard.

And many piker bullock through his cunning often missed,
Found himself quickly outsmarted by the pilot Peter Smith.

With that rarest combination that all the greats possess,
Of cattleman and pilot, of judgment and finesse.
In scrubs like hairs on dog's backs or out on open plains.
Whether quiet cow or wild bull, the results they never changed.

Every bit his reputation and nothing of a myth,
Yet down to earth and friendly was the pilot Peter Smith.

Watercolour on paper by Earl Robinson

I remember when we lost him, flying back to shut a gate.
His family lost a father, and the stockman lost a mate.
And so many bush kids saddened who he'd taken for a flight,
Yet they dreamed of flying choppers when they fell asleep at night.

And those of them who followed, if granted just one wish,
Would ask for half the measure of the pilot Peter Smith.

These days there seem so many choppers buzzing in the sky,
That I joke in contemplation how they surely don't collide.
But they're just part of the framework of the picture of the song,
Of the story of the outback, as they bring the tail along.

And some are bloody useless, and some would seem to have a gift,
But I still ain't seen the equal of the pilot Peter Smith.

Oil on canvas by Min Jones

The Old Ringer and the Gun

The gun stood five foot nine, he was stocky built and young,
And he'd done a lot of skiting 'bout the fighting that he'd done:
How many men had tried him, but none were yet to stand;
His speed that rivalled lighting and the power of his right hand.

The Old Ringer's hair was greying, his legs were bent and bowed,
And his youth and prime behind him now so many years ago.
But he'd grown up in the Outback, where you don't back down or run,
So, he stood his ground that morning, when he locked horns with the Gun.

Now the Gun's mates gathered 'round him, they knew he'd win the fight:
He'd show that old bloke something; he'd soon switch out the lights.
But I had myself an inkling, that might not be the way it goes,
For while the gun he stood flat footed, that old ringer's on his toes.

Well, the Gun shaped up and walked in as he threw the opening punch,
But the Old Ringer blocked and countered, and it landed with a crunch.
The Gun couldn't believe it as he crawled up from the dirt:
It must have been a lucky punch, but bloody hell it hurt!

But he had his pride and honour, and reputation to defend.
He shaped up and threw the right, but that luck it struck again.
He wasn't sure he liked this much, but he had to have a go:
So, he got up once again and he swung a mighty blow.

But the Old Ringer he just ducked him, and its' force spun him around.
The Gun had only been hit twice, but three times he'd been down.
But he came up for another, and once more he got floored,
And this time he was certain: he didn't want to fight no more.

His face was sore and battered, through the blood and dirt and tears.
It wasn't quite like fighting on a bar stool with a beer.
And when he finally got his wind back, no more the mighty Gun,
He hit his pins and bolted, like a scalded cat would run.

Now I've been around the country, and seen a fair few blues:
Some tough and rumble stoushes; been in the odd one too.
But I don't recall a knuckle up I've watched was so much fun,
As the day that Old Ringer knocked the fight out of the Gun.

So, here's a little caution to you would-be loud mouthed louts:
Be a little wary of those old blokes in the bush who get about,
'Cause they might have done some fighting in the "days of long ago",
And they might just show you something about the grass you didn't know.

'And We Boil the Quart Pots,' charcoal on canvas by Katie Jones

Riding Evil Eden for the Lead

In the Normanby ranges, where the mountains swiftly climb,
From the farming plains of Bowen there below,
In country rough and rugged where angels fear to tread,
And even fools are seldom known to go –

You may see me there a-riding where the granite outcrops break,
Through the hills and gullies fast, at breakneck speed.
For I have no fear of falling on the loose and rocky ground,
When I'm riding Evil Eden for the lead.

Through the Quinine and the Ironbarks, over fallen Morten Ash,
Past twisted ridges lined with Bloodwood trees,
Where the fastest river flows from the Hawkstone up above,
And the ghosts of miners past run wild and free.

oil on canvas by Kath Pemble

Where the wily agile Brahman who've made these hills his own,
Is a smart and cunning adversary indeed.
But the odds are quickly evened in this game of cat and mouse,
When I'm riding Evil Eden for the lead.

Just a wild-eyed creamy gelding, snorty, snake, and game,
The kind that takes a horseman just to ride.
But his sins are soon forgiven in the Cocky Apple scrubs,
And the Tea Tree soaks, where cleanskin mickeys hide.

A throwback to an era when the fences numbered few,
When horses of his type were much in need.
Though this kind have all but vanished, I'm glad a few remain,
When I'm riding Evil Eden for the lead.

'Riding Evil Eden for the Lead' oil on canvas by Katie Jones

See, I grew up in the desert, in the Wattle learned to ride,
Through the Gidgee and False Sandalwood at pace.
And I've worked up in the basalt where the sons of Truly Brave,
Through the holes and rocky ground were born to race.

But out upon these mountains a man can come to grief,
If the lessons of this land he fails to heed.
Yet I can hold the best of local ringers born and bred,
When I'm riding Evil Eden for the lead.

The crowds may flock to Flemington to see the Thoroughbred,
And the jockeys for the cup a-riding hard.
But this racetrack's ever changing and the finish line's defined,
At the day's end by the cattle in the yard.

Where I doubt the great Bart Cummings with his victories and fame,
Would dare to back his best and fastest steed.
And I wouldn't give the Diva half of Buckley's chance,
At racing Evil Eden for the lead.

Riding hard to bend a bullock, or to ring the leaders round,
When horses tire, and best of dogs are beat.
With his spring-like legs beneath him, and ears pricked to the chase,
I am yet to feel the stumble of his feet.

And I hold some apprehension for the day I know will come,
When from these wild ranges I secede.
And I won't be half the ringer or as handy as I look
When I'm riding Evil Eden for the lead.

Oil on canvas by Kath Pemble

The Song the Hobble Chains Sang

This is the song the hobble chains sang, when the last drover hung up his rains.
And this is the tune of a Condamine bell, with the plant horses turned out to graze.
This is the noise a packsaddle makes, as it hangs gathering dust,
And the silent cry of the bits and the spurs, as time slowly turns then to rust.

This is the sigh that the boss drover sighed, as he watched the roadtrains roll by.
And the tears that flowed free in the horse tailer's heart, as he watched all he knew slowly die.
And this is a song of an era that's gone, and boys, it ain't coming back.
But it's ghost may be heard as it pushes the mob, through the heat down a dry dusty track.

watercolour by Earl Robinson

This is the drum of the relentless rain, and a swag that never would dry.
And of horses that bucked on a cold winter's morning and made for one hell of a ride.
This is the echo of the bullocks that rushed, at night on the hard broken ground.
And the clatter of hooves as the ringers they rode, through the scrub trying to wheel them around.

This is the clang that the cranky old cook, on the side of his camp oven made.
And the cornbeef and damper you ate by the fire, at the end of another long day.
And this is a song of an era that's gone, and boys, it ain't coming back.
But it's ghost may be heard as the hobble chains sing, through the heat down a dry dusty track.

watercolour on paper by Earl Robinson

Neville Jingle and the Bronco Horse

This is a story my father tells,
So many times that I know it well,
Where the gulf rivers run on Augustus Downs,
Back in his youth in the long-ago-now.

"The manager then was old Graham White,
Who with tucker was stingy and pay just as tight,
So, I lied 'bout my years when I told him my age.
So the miserable bugger would pay me full wage."

"My mate Wonnie Neilson back then ran the camp,
Horses and swags and the old bronco ramp,
Not that long since they'd dropped the act,
And most of the stockmen in those days were black."

"And the best of the crew, who could stake his claim,
Was a young Doomagee fella, Jingle by name,
And I swear that before or since where I've been,
A better man at riding buckjumpers I've never seen."

Oil on canvas by Kath Pemble

"Now the main bronco horse was a big solid gray,
Of Percheron blood who would work hard all day,
A big sappy weaner, a wild cow, a mickey, or bull,
Was nothing that big horse couldn't pull."

"Such fine work of art when those two were combined,
And a better team yet I would doubt you could find,
On a green hide rope, if you scoured the whole land.
Than that big grey horse and that tall dark-skinned man."

"On a Gutta-Percha swamp where the ground was hard,
On a near treeless flat stood the old bronco yards,
And it's tied hard and fast when you're branding in this way'
With green hide to collar by an old hobble chain."

"Well this day it had started no different to most,
With Jingle in his place on the end of a rope,
When he caught a big weaner and pulled upon the slack,
But it came up high and the green hide fell back."

Watercolour on paper by Earl Robinson

"In behind of his neck and it pulled him on down,
But he wasn't so lucky as to land on the ground,
Well the grey headed out with the ramp on his mind,
With our poor mate Neville hung up in the iron."

"The calf then decided as he followed in toe,
That round in behind was the best place to go,
And the rope it caught up under that big horse's tail,
Like the laws of old Murphy just couldn't fail."

"The grey started to buck, bloody hell he jumped high,
He hit that ground hard, and he kicked at the sky,
We rushed in to help him, but it seemed there was naught
We could do, for this young native ringer was caught."

"Till at last he came free, from behind of that rope,
But it wasn't the saving, we all might have hoped,
For his foot was still wedged tight, in that stirrup iron,
Straight out of the camp oven, right into the fire."

"Hanging up by his leg, as his head hit the ground,
And there he stayed swinging, till those hind feet came down,
Square on his chest landed, with an almighty clout,
And the force of the blow pulled his foot clean on out."

"He lay there so still as we all rushed to his aid,
And carried him to the only available shade,
On that treeless flat meant a bronco yard post,
This blackfella I swear looked as white as a ghost.

"We propped a coat beneath him for resting his head,
Had he been a white man, I'm sure that he'd be dead,
But times were harder back then, and life was rough,
And the Doomagee boys in those days were bred tough."

"Now I've seen horses buck, and I've seen ringers ride,
As I've travelled the north end of this country wide,
But I've not seen another like happened that day,
With Neville Jingle and the broncoing grey."

'Bronco Yard,' watercolour on paper by Earl Robinson

Back When the Horses Could Buck

Take me back to the days when my grandfather rode,
And this country was still free and wide.
On a big thoroughbred, in an old poly saddle,
With a good cattle dog by his side.

Fences where few and good men were plenty,
And hard through the timber they'd ride.
Wheeling the lead and backing you up,
Back in the days long gone by.

When a man was a man, and this land was a land,
Wild rugged untamed and rough.
You lived in the saddle, the hobble chains rattled,
Back when the horses could buck.

Mustering, these days, is all Jackaroos and lanes,
Watching the choppers bring them in.
But if I could find the road, I'd ride back in time
To a time when the horse was still king.

Oil on canvas by Min Jones

Cornbeef and damper, camped in your swag,
Under that old Southern cross.
I wonder some days if the comforts we've gained,
Are worth all the good things we've lost.

'Kieth,' charcoal on canvas by Earl Robinson

From when a man was a man, and this land was a land,
Wild rugged untamed and rough,
You lived in the saddle, the hobble chains rattled,
Back when the horses could buck.

When you rose in the morning to the old milky way,
Rode out with the gold morning light,
And boys trot along we've a long way to go,
Best we yard them before it turns night.

And the Mickies were wild as the ringers that chased,
With no choppers or catchers around.
You pumped him out, jumped off at full speed,
Grabbed his tail and pulled him to ground.

When a man was a man, and this land was a land,
Wild rugged untamed and rough,
You lived in the saddle the hobble chains rattled,
Back when the horses could buck.

No airconditioned quarters, no tv's back then,
Just a fire and a log cabin smoke.
And you told stories of the good men you've known,
Bad horses and cracked a few jokes.

And you ate what was cooked, drank your tea and retired,
To your bed on hard open ground.
And you dreamt of the rum and you dreamt of the girls
That you'd see on your next time in town.

When a man was a man, and this land was a land,
Wild rugged untamed and rough,
You lived in the saddle the hobble chains rattled,
Back when the horses could buck.

Watercolour on paper by Earl Robinson

Breakers Nightmare

I used to travel 'cross the outback breaking horses for crust,
Come rain, shine and hail storm, through mud, and fly and dust.
From gulf side of the 'ninchlar,' out on the big run for a time.
If you've been around there's a chance you've worked a colt of mine.

For company and private, for the ringer, kids and roo.
There were none I ever turned down, none I wouldn't do.
Buck, bite, strike and light out: young, old, wild or tame.
It didn't make much difference, to me they're all the same.

I never feared a single horse, he had his job, I had mine.
And for the most part of the contract, we'd get along just fine.
For it's not the snaky bastards that'll drive you to your beer,
Fills your dreams with nightmares, makes a tough man quake in fear.

'Whaler,' charcoal on canvas by Katie Jones

To every contract breaker, there's a time you learn to dread.
That makes you wake in nervous sweats, a-thrashing in your bed.
See you'll take a mob, you'll break 'em, but before you get your pay,
You must pass a bloody mine field that they call hand over day.

Now, this day was based entirely on the law that Murphy penned.
And stupidity the constant, that you surely can depend.
I'm not sure if by management, inbreeding or plain luck
The skill that some possesses, to make the quietest buck.

There's always the great whisperer, who can barely ride a horse;
A self-proclamated expert, knows far more then you of course.
Then there's the nervous shakers, and the pocket knives half shut,
Make you wish for shot-o-Bundy for the churning in your gut.

But you keep a calm and gentle voice; ride all the colts with ease.
Smile and give encouragement; try your very best to please.
"Talk to 'im", "Move about 'im" "Let 'im know you're here."
You wonder if they're deaf, or foreign, or maybe not all there.

You show 'em, then you tell 'em, but nothing seems to sink.
Like some allergy to horses, that makes 'em unable to think.
"Do it this way," "See like this mate and it'll go along just fine."
"Okay, I must speak for entertainment, don't you pay me any mind".

There's the ones who will get better, the ones who never will,
And the serial offenders, who you'd love the chance to kill.
The know-alls and special people, with their specialness abound.
The jumped-up Jillaroos that you'd really love to drown.

So give me colts with fiery-eyes, run from the pits of hell.
I'll take 'em on, I'll do my best to break the buggers well.
But could I draft the jockeys? Pick who comes; who stays away?
And I might just save my sanity, come next hand over day.

The Saddle and the Spur

The fenceline stretches onward,
As the hot sun beats on down.
I curse the flies, as I drive
Steel in rocky ground.
And my mind, it starts to wander,
To a life I used to know.
And I'm once again a younger man,
Oh it seems so long ago.

When I travelled 'cross this country,
Breaking horses for a crust.
From Tully rains, to Barkley plains,
In the mud and wind and dust.
Sometimes I close my eyes at night,
When I feel the west wind blow.
My mind goes back, down memories track,
To a life I used to know.

Oil on canvas by Kath Pemble

And I'm beating down a dusty track,
In my Holden Kingswood ute.
Pushing pedal to the metal,
In my size ten Blundstone boots.
With no one there beside me,
'Cept my old red mangy cur.
When a man could make a living,
With the saddle and the spur.

Old Luke, my dog, his luck ran out,
In the hills that fatal day.
And I suppose, that's how life goes,
But I was miles away.
Traveling 'cross some foreign country,
I guess I rambled till I found.
A mate for life, to be my wife,
Had kids and settled down.

Oil on canvas by Min Jones

40

These days I'm contract fencing,
In these rolling basalt hills.
The going's tough, the fenceline's rough ,
But the money pays the bills.
And though I wouldn't trade my old life back,
For my wife and family.
Still I reminisce, of times I miss
When I was young and free.

And I'm beating down a dusty track,
In my Holden Kingswood ute.
Pushing pedal to the metal,
In my size ten Blundstone boots.
With no one there beside me,
'Cept my old red mangy cur.
When a man could make a living,
With the saddle and the spur.

'On the Tail,' charcoal on canvas by Katie Jones

Scotty

In the spring of '09, up in Alberta,
To the town of Longview I happened to go.
Out on the big loop, snowed in by a blizzard,
Up in the foot hills where High River flows.

There an old cowboy, he told me the stories,
Days of his youth and the life he had known.
When first he drifted, from his homeland in Scotland,
To the plains down under oh for to roam.

The life of a ringer, who moved the big mobs,
Cutting out bullocks, on an open face camp.
Packhorse and damper, Bronco horse pulling,
A wild eyed young Micky, up to the ramp.

The hard bred stockhorse, the dark western stockman,
The eerie min min, that shines in the night.
Heatwaves dancing, parched cracks of black soil,
Bush towns and women, the rum and the fights.

And he talked about horses and he talked about cattle.
On the west Queensland plains, and his life in the saddle.
Where the rain never falls, and the channels in flood,
Of the dust and the flies, and the old Gidgee Bug.

watercolour on paper by Earl Robinson

43

The winds of knowing came once more a blowing,
Carried him off to the cold northern land.
Out there in the Rockies, with a horn on his saddle,
Making a living with a rope in his hand.

Branding and calving, the Gang Ranch, the Bar U,
Packing and wrangling on the divide.
Rounding up in the springtime, the smell of brands burning,
Riding the herd around calving time.

And he talked about horses and he talked about cattle.
Of mountains, the prairies, and his life in the saddle.
The foothills and cabins where the tall pine trees grow.
The snow drifts melting, when the Chinook winds blow.

Hands hard and broken, the lines of hard living,
Had burned like a brand into his hide.
Then he rolled up a smoke, sipped his black coffee,
And stared at the Rockies with his faded old eyes.

So, let's talk about horses and talk about cattle.
Of mountains and plains and life in the saddle.
When dust storms blow and the rivers run wide.
And sing of the horseman, wherever he rides.

'The Cascades,' oil on canvas by Katie Jones

44

The Horse I Couldn't Sell

We bought him in some doggers, some good few years on back.
Just an ugly, pouched mouth, half blind, mule-eared looking black.
If you're describing ugly, he'd have been the name you said.
The type of horse the poodles and the bird eaters are fed
Narrow gauged, capped hipped and weedy, it wasn't hard to tell
With his head the only thing of size, he'd be bloody hard to sell.

They said that he'd been broken in but I was soon to find
A difference in their definition of broken in – to mine.
There's different ways to skin a cat, it's not who's wrong or right.
But he reared when you turned him left and he locked up to the right.
And we ran some "hot discussions" that concluded I was boss.
And to challenge that decision would result in further loss.

Watercolour on paper by Earl Robinson

And a buyer came to see them, and he looked from horse to horse.
He nodded and said, "I take them all, except the black of course.
I don't want that sort of rubbish; you'll have to pull him out.
I cannot fathom for my life who'd keep one like that about."
I wasn't disappointed, though I knew damn good and well.
That I would now be landed with a horse I couldn't sell.

There is something horsemen know, who chase the wild stock.
In the scrubs and mountain rangers through brigalow or rock.
A feeling in a horse's stride, though I can't explain it right.
The courage and persistence that's most needed in the fight.
For beauty does not matter when the days are long and hard.
And you're not paid for being pretty, but to get them in the yard.

Steel is forged in fire they say, well fire was what he found.
Bending spoilt bullocks in the basalt through holes and rocky ground
He would run and stop and pivot, though the scrubs of black Tea Trees.
As we rode hard to bend the waves back of this rolling Brahman sea.
But we kept the lead together and we steadied them as well.
Till I got them in the laneway on the horse I couldn't sell.

Wild cattle were the standard of his life right from the start.
What he lacked in the looks department he made up for in heart.
Blading bullocks twice his size, who'd charge and kick and hook.
Never quitting, never backing down, whatever that it took.
To yard the rouge'n cattle, who'd won too many times before.
When you give everything you have and still are needing more.

And now it seems the years of work have surely not been kind.
His joints have aged and stiffened and his bad eye's got more blind.
But his heart is still just as solid, and his courage never wanes.
Though I know he's nearly finished to admit it brings me pain
For to me he's more then priceless and I guess that you can tell.
I wouldn't part for Packers ransom, with the horse I couldn't sell.

Brawler of the Pen

I have made my lifelong study of the kings of rhyming verse.
To the point of mad obsession or some type of linguistic curse.
I have read and I have pondered 'til at last I've narrowed down
Those who could fitly lay a claim as such, to title and the crown.

In my deliberations it always comes back to one of three.
Paterson is best I'm sure but close behind is Lawson and Ogilvie.
I'd love to walk the footsteps upon the tracks of these great men.
But alas it seems, despite efforts best, I'm just a brawler of the pen.

How the words they write remind me of a boxer on his toes.
With ease and grace their combinations of the written verses flow.
How they duck, weave and counter, description, word and rhyme.
How they find that perfect meter's pace for their poetry sublime.

Did it really come to them so easily as their finished product seems?
Or did they have to labour hard, did it haunt their very dreams?
Did they write, rewrite and frustrate, then quit and start again?
Were they spared the limitations reserved for brawlers of the pen?

Oil on canvas by Min Jones

I have ridden in the eastern ranges where a slip could mean your death.
Where the broken ridges twisted and the boldest held their breath.
I have travelled those fabled sunlit plains, with sheep on western track.
I've sent my horse at galloping pace, on the timbered runs outback.

Through swamp and quicksand creeks, in wet back soil I've rode.
The gulf's wide flats to the gidgee scrubs and open plains I've known.
From the Kimberly to the Eastern coast, I have tramped back and again.
And despite all I've done and seen I'm still a brawler of the pen.

More time perhaps in the school room ring is what some would say.
But I could not be bound to wooden desk, like dogs to a spike all day.
For life I vowed could never live from the page of history books.
And if fact, it's worth a mention then surely, it's worth a look.

So there the life of the bush I chose, the life to which I was raised.
And to live its trials and write it tales, I resolved to spend my days.
To write on down what quickly passes of horse and beast and men.
In rough and ready fashion plied as such, just a brawler of the pen .

As I throw words blindly around, like haymakers from the hip.
With flurries lacking stance and structure mumbled from my lips.
Like some drunk who fights a shadow, for something that it said.
Or a pug who's only claim to fame is blocking with his head.

As I read Kendall and Gordon, McKellar, Dutton and Morant.
And try as best that I know how, to enrapture and enchant.
And I'd love to be remembered as a peer of these great men.
But alas it seems I'm just another brawler of the pen.

Oil painting by Kath Pemble

J. D. (Jet) Jones is the author of children's books 'Not Far to Go Now,' and 'Hard in the Yards.' He grew up in outback Queensland immersed in the culture and poetry of the bush. His poems depict his life mustering cattle, breaking in horses and building fences. He also writes songs, and has put his own and others stories to verse. This is his first book of bush poetry.

Katie Jones spent her formative years in Canada, coming to Australia in 2009. These days she calls rural North Queensland home, sharing her life with her husband J. D. (Jet) Jones and their three children. She is a professional artist and illustrator, and works primarily in charcoals, a medium that suits the dry, dusty subject matter she has made her specialty.

Min Jones started painting when her life was stretched to its fullest with the never ending workload associated with life on the land. Cooking for the station team, raising a family and teaching school, along with the numerous needs that come with remote and isolated living. The importance of taking a little time to do something creative to relax and refresh found her reaching for a paintbrush and a camera. Landscapes and old buildings took on a new life as she rekindled a fresh love for the beauty of the Australian bush.

Eva Luther has always enjoyed drawing animals and nature. As a small child, she would take a sketch pad and pencil and sit among the cattle in the paddock to quietly sketch them, up close and personal. Living on a cattle station in West Queensland she has had the wonderful advantage of being surrounded by a vast source of inspirational material. It is her hope that the passion and sentiment that moves her to create her workflows through to the viewers, giving them the experience of her reality.

Kath Pemble grew up on a cane farm in Home Hill, Queensland. It was here that she met and married a farmer and had the first five of their eventual six children. In the '70s the family made the transition to cattle and eventually settled on a station outside of Charters Towers. She learned much of her artistic craft from a teacher in Charters Towers, Mrs. Schluter. Kath Pemble works predominately in oils and pastels. Her work can be found at the Don Roderick Gallery, Charters Towers.

Earl Robinson may be the only stockman to have been born in a zoo: his family owned the Mount St. John Zoo in Townsville. He spent most of his working life in North Queensland, working on cattle stations as a stockman, before operating machinery in civil earthworks and mining. Earl Robinson taught himself to draw in the mid '90s to keep busy while he quit smoking. Earl's favourite medium is watercolour, along with pen and wash. His artwork hangs in homes and shops throughout Charters Towers and surrounds.

'Hobble Chains,' pencil on paper by Jet Jones